Yorkshire Dales: **Pub** Walks

Text: *Neil Coates*
Series editor: *Tony Bowerman*
Photographs: *Neil Coates, Mark Richards , Shutterstock, Dreamstime, Carl Rogers*

Design: *Carl Rogers*

© *Northern Eye Books Limited 2014*

Northern Eye Books

ISBN 978-1-908632-10-4

A CIP catalogue record for this book is available from the British Library.

www.northerneyebooks.co.uk

Important Advice: The routes described in this book are undertaken at the reader's own risk. Walkers should take into account their level of fitness, wear suitable footwear and clothing, and carry food and water. It is also advisable to take the relevant OS map with you in case you get lost and leave the area covered by our maps.

Whilst every care has been taken to ensure the accuracy of the route directions, the publishers cannot accept responsibility for errors or omissions, or for changes in the details given. Nor can the publisher and copyright owners accept responsibility for any consequences arising from the use of this book.

If you find any inaccuracies in either the text or maps, please write or email us at the address below. Thank you.

First published in 2014 by

Northern Eye Books Limited
Northern Eye Books, Tattenhall, Cheshire CH3 9PX

Email: tony@northerneyebooks.com

For sales enquiries, please call 01928 723 744

Cover: *Craven Arms, Appletreewick (Walk 6) Photo: Carl Rogers*

Contents

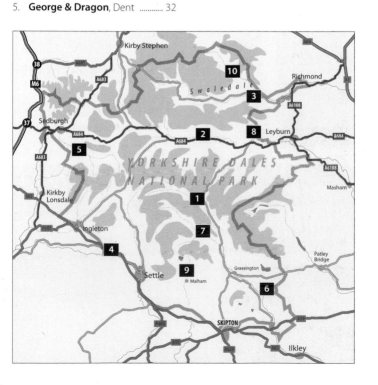

Pennine perfection

Designated in 1954, the **Yorkshire Dales** cover 1,762 square kilometres/680 square miles of the central Pennines. As well as some of Yorkshire's most magnificent landscapes, the National Park also includes a corner of Cumbria, where the secluded Howgill Fells loom over the River Lune. 'Dales' is something of a misnomer, for in addition to the beautiful dales the area incorporates great tracts of wild moorland, the famous 'Three Peaks' and an intriguing industrial heritage.

Over 1,300 miles of rights of way allow walkers to explore all facets of the Park. In addition, almost 110,000 hectares of open access land has opened up endless possibilities for exploring this heady mix of limestone and gritstone scenery. Upwards of 8 million visitors a year enjoy this striking countryside with its picturesque stone villages.

Stone barns and hay meadows in pretty Swaledale

Ales in the Dales

The pubs of the Yorkshire Dales reflect both the area and the local people: occasionally gritty and challenging, sometimes uncompromising but essentially hugely welcoming and full of character. Some of England's best watering holes stand here beside country lanes and village greens as they have for centuries past, gathering and exuding that unique amalgam which defines a pub. The flagged floors, the winter fires, the lamplight pooling onto lanes through bottle-glass windows, the quirky bars; that happy jigsaw of time and place which makes rambling to and between them one of life's great pleasures.

"There is nothing in which so much happiness is produced as a good tavern or inn".

Dr Samuel Johnson, c. 1760

TOP 10 **Walks:** The Dales' best Pub Walks

THE VILLAGE INN is at the heart of any community; a place for relaxation and gossip, reflection and camaraderie. Add a wealth of extraordinary countryside, a chance to challenge the outdoors and the promise of finely crafted local beers and you have a Dales experience bar-none. Those featured in this book reflect the perfect melding of boots and beer, a considered balance of the great outdoors and the great indoors — in a land for all seasons.

White Lion Inn
Cray
page 8

Rose & Crown Hotel AD 1445

Rose & Crown
Bambridge
page 14

The Buck Hotel
Reeth
page 20

New Inn
Clapham
page 26

The White Lion overlooks the lively Cray Gill

White Lion Inn, Cray

A classic valley and fellside walk in the Upper Wharfe Valley, with superb views and two pubs en-route

What to expect:
Field paths, back lanes and bridleways, one modest climb

Distance/time: 9km/ 5½ miles. Allow 3 hours

Start: Buckden National Park car park (pay & display)

Grid ref: SD 942 773

Ordnance Survey Map: Explorer OL30 Yorkshire Dales: *Northern & Central areas: Wensleydale & Swaledale*

The Pub: White Lion Inn, Cray, Skipton, North Yorkshire BD23 5JB | 01756 760262 | www.thewhitelioncray.com

Walk outline: From pretty Buckden, the Dales Way is joined on a riverside stretch to Hubberholme's ancient inn and church. Tracks and paths climb to higher limestone terraces with superb Wharfedale views before The White Lion detains prior to a waterfall-infused final section. The tracks and paths are generally well-used and signed. Mud in places.

Set in memorable limestone countryside beside a tributary of the River Wharfe, the **White Lion Inn** *is an old drovers' inn that oozes character and antiquity, with stone-flagged floors, open fires, oak beams and colourwashed stone walls, plus two small rooms served from an up-steps bar.*

Unusual pub game

▶ White Lion Inn at a glance

Open: Daily 10am-11pm

Brewery/company: Free house

Real ales: Timothy Taylor Golden Best, Copper Dragon Golden Pippin and Best Bitter, John Smith Cask

Food: Daily 12-2pm, 6-8.30pm. Good, solid, home-cooked pub fare using Dales meat, fish and cheese. Try the filled Yorkshire puds, or the changing specials board

Rooms: Nine rooms en-suite

Outside: Tables to front overlook Cray Gill waterfalls

Children & dogs: Children and dogs welcome

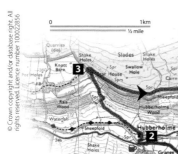

The Walk

1. Leave the car park and head towards the village; then turn right beside the green along **Dubb's Lane**. Cross the **River Wharfe** before turning right through a handgate, joining the waymarked **Dales Way** footpath, initially upstream beside the river and with a seasonal wealth of birds (look for dippers, kingfishers and wagtails) and wildflowers. The well-used path drifts back to the lane; turn right to gain **The George Inn**, at one end of the old bridge in the tiny village of **Hubberholme**.

The George Inn is, on the first Monday night of each year, the location for an archaic auction called the Hubberholme Parliament. Glebe land, belonging to the church, is let to the local farmer who has tabled the highest bid during the burn-time of a candle lit by the vicar in the dining room. The bidders remain in the bar and are thus unable to see the candle. The money raised goes to help the parish poor.

The writer JB Priestley was a regular patron at this ancient inn; his ashes are in the churchyard at nearby St Michael & All Angels Church, just across the bridge. The renowned craftsman Robert "Mouseman" Thompson supplied much of the church furniture; see if you can spot his trademark carved mice on the pews. The church also retains an extremely rare pre-Reformation rood loft.

2. Cross the bridge and take the fingerposted farm lane beside the churchyard wall, bend left behind the

Dales farm: *Hay Close huddles in tree-lined Cray Gill*

church and then stay on the wide, surfaced track, rising to the remote buildings at the imposing **Scar House**, nowadays a holiday let.

There's a Quaker burial ground beneath the four gigantic sycamore trees to the left of the cattle byres here. George Fox, founder of the Society of Friends of the Truth (later known as the Quakers) preached here surreptitiously in 1652 and again in 1677. Quakerism was illegal until 1689 and James Tennant, the Scar House farmer who first hosted Fox, was jailed for his religious convictions and died in York gaol in 1674.

3. Slip between the house and barn, curling left a short way up the track to a mossy fingerpost for 'Cray'. Turn right on a gently rising path that can be slippery underfoot across the bare limestone. Passing by the vast old spreading sycamores, the way shortly levels as a contour path around the flank of **Slades Hill**, with the oaks of **Hubberholme Wood** beyond the wall on your right, at first obscuring the views south.

Upland mosaic: *Drystone walls pattern the hillside above Upper Wharfedale*

Where the woods thin and peel back, one of the best lowland views in the Yorkshire Dales is revealed; a magnificent prospect across Upper Wharfedale, dappled with a patchwork of walled fields and stone barns slumbering below the enclosing round-shouldered fells, clipped by sharp edges and cut by tumbling becks.

The path slips along the hillside, climbing slightly across exposed limestone blocks and paralleling a wall to your right. Simply remain on the walked path, presently crossing a tree-shaded footbridge over **Cross Gill**.

Once through a gate beside a barn, drop with the developing field-road to pass behind the **White Lion Inn** to the adjacent road.

4. Walk up the road (be alert for vehicles on this short B-road stretch) above the waterfall-strewn gill; go round the right-hand bend and use the waymarked gate on the right. The field track is obvious, drifting left to pass through a **ford** beside a wall. Look up to your left here; in wetter weather **Cow Close Gill** plunges over a series of waterfalls here on the northern flanks of **Buckden Pike**.

The smooth, undulating profile of Buckden Pike disguises a turbulent history of mining.

In the hill-folds above the higher waterfalls is the site of Bishopdale Gavel Lead Mine; whilst high above Buckden car park, the deep gash of Buckden Beck hides many remnants of Buckden Gavel Lead Mine, worked from the 1600s until around 1880.

5. The track, occasionally gated, develops into a pre-turnpike fell-road, **Buckden Rake**, which drops back to the edge of the car park at **Buckden**. ♦

Drovers' Inns

Inns such as the White Lion developed to serve drovers. These hardy souls were hired to herd cattle, sheep, horses and geese along wide grassy tracks from the upland pastures of northern England and Wales to the markets of the growing industrial cities. They broke their journeys at inns offering sustenance; the animals were corralled in adjoining pens or paddocks. Drovers disappeared in the early 1900s, when rail transport finally replaced them.

A sunny summer's afternoon outside the Rose & Crown

Rose & Crown, Bainbridge

Along a Roman Road to the moors before reaching a secluded lake and England's shortest river

What to expect:
Rough tracks, lanes and riverside meadows, one long steady climb

Distance/time: 8.5km/ 5¼ miles. Allow 3 hours

Start/finish: Bainbridge; roadside parking beside the greens

Grid ref: SD 934 903

Ordnance Survey Map: Explorer OL30 Yorkshire Dales: *Northern & Central areas: Wensleydale & Swaledale*

The Pub: Rose & Crown Hotel, Bainbridge, Wensleydale, North Yorkshire DL8 3EE | 01969 650735 | www.theprideofwensleydale.co.uk

Walk outline: The old Roman road rises gradually from Bainbridge's green heart, heading towards the imposing, flat-topped Wether Fell and revealing a great sweeping view of higher Wensleydale before falling into secluded Raydale. Remote Semer Water and the pretty hamlet of Countersett prelude a riverside return beside the River Bain beneath the shoulder of stately Addlebrough.

Originally built in 1445, this low, whitewashed inn fronts the huge village greens. The public bar is a hive of activity and popular with the locals; compact old rooms warmed by fires are an ideal retreat for ramblers fresh off the moors.

Snooker lounge

▶ The Rose & Crown Hotel at a glance

Open: Daily 11am-11pm
Brewery/company: Free house
Real ales: Theakston's, Black Sheep
Food: Monday-Friday 12 noon-2.30pm & 6-9pm; weekends 12 noon-4pm & 6-9pm (8pm Sun); famous for local meats and roasts
Rooms: Eleven en-suite rooms
Outside: Tables overlook the village greens
Children & dogs: Children and dogs welcome

The Walk

1. Put your back to the **Rose & Crown** and head half-right, across the upper green and over the main road onto the village lane signed for 'Countersett and Semer Water'. Look across the grassy width of the immense central green; beyond the cottages and the **River Bain** is the low hillock of **Brough Hill**.

The Roman fort of Virosidum was built on Brough Hill, immediately east of the village, for General Agricola in the 1st century AD. It acted as a base for controlling the Celtic Brigantes tribe whose lands the Romans took and as a supervisory centre for lead mining in the general area. It was one of the longest-lasting Roman forts, surviving until the early 5th Century.

Turn right at the head of the green, past the **Old Hall** and commence a steady climb out of Bainbridge. At the sharp left bend in 1 kilometre, leave the tarred lane in favour of the rougher track branching ahead.

This is Cam High Road, the old Roman Road linking Bainbridge to Ingleton. In the 18th century it was the main turnpike linking Richmond to Lancaster and, as such, one of the main trans-Pennine roads of the Georgian era. In all, the road has been in use for 1900 years.

It's an unforgiving steady climb, tempered by rest

Rock of ages: *A traditional stone barn with Addlebrough Hill on the horizon*

stops to enjoy the huge views into the highest reaches of Wensleydale, beyond the church tower at Hawes visible in the near-distance. As you reach a point opposite-below the sharp snouted **Countersett Crag** to your left, look carefully for a small handgate on your left.

2. Take this and head half-left up the rough pasture on a discernible path, aiming for the point where the wall disappears over the skyline. (If you miss this path, simply turn left up the tarred lane you'll shortly meet). Turn left on the lane; as it bends right, downhill, take the path left for 'Countersett', hugging the wall to cross a lower stile. Beyond this **Semer Water** becomes visible below in **Raydale**. In 100 metres bear left across the pasture, passing below a fenced enclosure and then through a stile in-line with the barn. Drop well-right of the barn to use stiles across a beck, then rise past the fingerpost before dropping to a gate into a rough lane. Go ahead to **Countersett**.

Sky mirror: *Semer Water reflects the deep azure blue of a cloudless spring sky*

3. Slip right, then left downhill for **Stalling Busk**. Cross the **old Bain Bridge**; your route is left, but take time to visit the nearby lake of **Semer Water**.

The legend of Semer Water concerns a drowned city. It was cursed by a saint who was refused bread and board by all of the wealthy inhabitants; overnight the city sank beneath the water and only the poor shepherd's family who did offer him succour were saved. Remains of an Iron Age settlement have been discovered in the lake sediments.

4. Follow the path downstream beside the **River Bain**. Beyond a footbridge and nearby ladder-stile, drift right away from the water on a well-walked path. A series of narrow handgates take you up left of the higher stone barn, climbing then to a grassy hill-lip high above the Bain's wooded gorge.

The River Bain drains Semer Water to the River Ure, joining it just north of Bainbridge. Its measured length of just 4 kilometres (2½ miles) means it is the shortest river in England.

5. To your right is the distinctive flat-topped hill of **Addlebrough**. Keep

ahead on a wide grassy trod beyond a further handgate, dropping to parallel a lane on your right. Keep downhill within the field, presently enjoying the view down across the old mill at Bainbridge. Nowadays, the water drives not mill-wheels but an Archimedean Screw, generating electricity for 40 village homes. A narrow stile gives into the main road; turn left to the village to complete the walk. ♦

Rare natural lake

Semer Water is one of only two natural lakes in the Yorkshire Dales (the other is Malham Tarn) and owes its existence to the last glaciation. The ice sheet retreated, leaving a moraine, or ridge, that dammed the valley south of Wensleydale. The present lake is the remnant of a much larger water that once all-but filled Raydale. Today, the lake is a nature reserve that supports summer water lilies, whooper swans and great crested grebes.

The characterful Buck Hotel, in Reeth

The Buck Hotel, Reeth

Saunter on the moors above the Swale to lead-mining heritage and a cracking riverside return

Distance/time: 11km/ 7 miles. Allow 3½ - 4 hours

Start/finish: Reeth

Grid ref: SE 037 993

Ordnance Survey Map: Explorer OL30 Yorkshire Dales: *Northern & Central areas: Wensleydale & Swaledale*

The Pub: The Buck Hotel, Reeth, Swaledale, North Yorkshire DL11 6SW | 01748 884210 | www.buckhotel.co.uk

What to expect:
Mostly good paths and tracks, several short climbs, boggy patches, some narrow gap stiles

Walk outline: From Reeth's massive green the walk eases up to the fringe of Low Moor and a firm trod below Calver Hill, with an extensive panorama over Swaledale to the ridge of Gibbon Hill and High Carl. Dropping into Mill Gill, gaunt ruins remain of the lead-mining industry hereabouts. Descending by Barney Beck Woods to tiny Healaugh, the Swale is then joined downstream to return to Reeth.

The Buck Hotel's *pedigree as a Georgian coaching inn is evident in the nooks, crannies and blazing fire of the homely bar and snug. The locally popular game of quoits is fascinating to watch, on pitches in the enclosed beer garden.*

THE
BUCK HOTEL
~ AT REETH ~
circa 1770
~~
10 En-Suite Bedrooms
Good Home Cooked Food
Quality Cask Ales

The writing's on the wall

▶ The Buck Hotel at a glance

Open: Open daily, 11am-midnight (may vary slightly)
Brewery/company: Free House
Real ales: Copper Dragon, Tim Taylor, Black Sheep and microbreweries, with 3 real ciders
Food: Daily 12noon-3pm & 6pm-9pm Swaledale produce to the fore, with some great specials. Home-made pizzas until 11.30pm
Rooms: Ten en-suite rooms
Outside: Large hidden beer garden, patio tables overlook the green
Children & dogs: Children and dogs welcome

The Walk

1. Facing **The Buck Hotel**, turn left for Gunnerside along **Silver Street**.

The 'capital' of upper Swaledale, picturesque Reeth evolved as a centre for stocking knitting, worth £40,000 in 1823, equivalent to £3.3 million today. Local lore has it that miners even knitted whilst walking to and from the mine-workings higher up Swaledale, in order to eke out a living. The mines, first recorded in Roman times, were lead-mines; profit from these paid for some of the imposing houses fringing the huge green — for the mine owners, not the miners. The village also held a thriving market, first chartered in 1695 when it usurped nearby Grinton's corn and linen market. The Swaledale Folk Museum, off the green, has some excellent information and displays about the village's heritage.

In 350 metres, turn right up the walled track of **Skelgate Lane**, twisting with this (ignore the gated fork left onto Riddings Farm's drive) to the end-gate onto open moorland. Advance here beside the wall; then go forward on the path, shortly joining a wider track at a bend. Keep ahead for 1.5 kilometres, passing above the top-most walled pastures here at the edge of **Reeth Low Moor**. Beyond the next set of fields the track drops past a cottage to a T-Junction at **Thirns** farmhouse.

This area can be excellent for bird-spotting. Of particular note are ring ouzels – like a

Lead shed?: *The ruins of Surrender Bridge smelting mill*

blackbird with a white bib, wheatears and golden plover, all specialists of moorland areas, as are the comical red grouse and the tiny merlin falcon.

2. Turn right and then fork right up the lesser track in 200 metres. Remain with this undulating, occasionally boggy and deteriorating moorland track across the flank of shapely **Calver Hill** for a further 1.25 kilometres, skirting above more walled pastures on your left. At the extreme far end of these use the bridlegate and drop with the path through the deep gill at **Cringley Bottom**. Ascending the steep, zigzag path beyond the flat bridge will soon bring you to ruined buildings spread above **Old Gang Beck**.

The ruins here are of Surrender Bridge smelting mill, built in 1841 and replacing earlier buildings dating back to the 1600's. This is where the galena ore, which had already been 'dressed' to remove most of the non-metalliferous rock, was melted and cast into ingots of lead; greatly

Heavy metal past: *The bridge, smelting mill and dressing sheds above Old Gang Beck*

increasing value and easing onward movement. The fuel would have been coal from small pits high on the moors and peat, dried and stored in long, pillared buildings such as the one of which scant remains are visible just above the smelting mill.

3. Find the sandy return path heading east (downstream) from the higher ruins. This skims the lip of the gorge; then drops steeply to cross the side-stream of **Bleaberry Gill**. Use the small handgate opposite; beyond this a thin path rises

gently to become a below-wall route along the edge of the wildflower-rich woods clothing **Barney Beck**. In 500 metres this enters the wood-top pasture via a thin stile; simply keep the wall close to your right. Way below a remote cottage, successive very narrow gap-stiles lead the path ahead into the woods, becoming a firm dirt track and then a surfaced driveway to reach a minor road.

4. Turn left to and through the hamlet of **Healaugh**. As the buildings peter out beside the small green, slip right beyond **Park Lodge cottage** on the finger-posted path to the riverside.

5. Turn downstream, accompanying the **Swale** for 1.5 kilometres to reach the suspension footbridge. Don't cross it; instead curve left up the well-walked path, turning right 100 metres above the

barn. Continue along the enclosed lane which leads back into nearby **Reeth**, to complete the walk. ◆

Underground, Overground

The atmospheric remains at Surrender Bridge were part of the Duke of Wharton's enterprises beside Old Gang Beck. Ores won from mines higher on the moors were smelted here; some was even moved underground from mines in Gunnerside Gill, 5 kilometres to the west. Most of the lead was sent by packhorse to Stockton-on-Tees for shipping around the country. The last Swaledale mine closed in 1912.

The three-storey New Inn looms over Clapham Beck

New Inn, Clapham

A memorable walk exploring the flanks of Ingleborough, Crummackdale and the Norber Stones glacial oddities

What to expect:
Largely firm paths and fell roads. Muddy and slippery in places.

Distance/time: 10.5km/ 6½ miles, allow 3½-4 hours

Start: Clapham village, National Park car park

Grid ref: SD 745 693

Ordnance Survey Map: Explorer OL2 Yorkshire Dales: *Southern & Western areas: Whernside, Ingleborough & Pen-y-ghent*

The Pub: The New Inn, Clapham, nr. Settle, North Yorkshire LA2 8HH | 01524 251203 | www.newinn-clapham.co.uk

Walk outline: Shapely Ingleborough rises north of Clapham. This walk traces Clapdale north along the skirts of the mountain, passing Ingleborough Cave and Trow Gill before rising over Long Scar to secluded Crummackdale, with its fabulous views to Moughton Scar. A final flourish visits the remarkable Norber Stones, stranded on wildflower-rich limestone pavement high above Austwick.

*An imposing three-storey Georgian edifice, The **New Inn** overlooks the beck in the centre of the village. Inside, caving cartoons reflect the handy location of the inn for some of England's most renowned underground systems.*

Dales' ales

▶ The New Inn at a glance

Open: Daily 11am-midnight
Brewery/company: Free House
Real ales: Regular Copper Dragon Golden Pippin, guests from Hawkshead, Moorhouses and other northern microbreweries
Food: All day from breakfast to 9.30pm. Solid menu of favourites plus thoughtfully created dishes mostly using local produce.
Rooms: Nineteen rooms all en suite
Outside: Paved patio to the rear, tables above the beck at front
Children & dogs: Children welcome; dogs in garden

The Walk

1. Turn right from the car park; keep left at the church, cross the beck and turn right, then left past the entrance gates to **Clapham Dale**. In another 200 metres go right on the rougher lane for 'Ingleborough'.

2. At the remote farmhouse at **Clapdale** go through the farmyard and turn right down to a rough lane. Turn left; shortly passing **Ingleborough Cave**, one of England's largest. Cross the **packhorse bridge** over the source of **Clapham Beck** and advance up the valley. As the track bends left, note the ladder-stile on your right; this is the onward route. First, however, walk round the bend up into the wooded chasm of **Trow Gill**.

One camp suggests that it was formed underground by water sinking through fissures, creating a cave system that then collapsed, exposing the gorge to weathering.

The waters became diverted along other fissures, which today are Ingleborough Cave. The other theory is that, when the great ice-sheets melted 12,000 years ago, the immensely powerful meltwaters tore down into the limestone plateau, forming Trow Gill.

3. Return to the ladder stile and tackle the steep pasture to a higher stile. Turn left along the track to a gate into open country. Turn right; then drift left to use a higher gate.

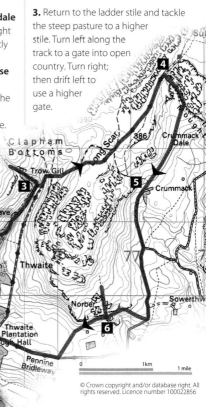

© Crown copyright and/or database right. All rights reserved. Licence number 100022856

Rocky road: *Two walkers pause in the limestone country above Beggar's Stile*

Continue up to the offset wall corner. Keep ahead on the stony track another 50 metres before sliding right on a grassy path to the large cairn on the skyline. Pass just right of this; in another 400 metres keep left at two adjacent forks, putting a limestone outcrop on your left. Off to your right, Pen-y-Ghent rises beyond the spectacular Moughton Scar limestone pavements beyond Crummack Dale. Beyond another large cairn a broken wall appears up on your left; then shortly a high wall on your right. Trace this to **Sulber Gate**, but not through it.

4. Use the small handgate on your right and drop down the steep path to the foot of the cliffs. Keep ahead 100 metres; then drift right along a rough path through the boulders and **limestone pavement**. *Moughton Scar's astonishing pavement originated beneath a glacier. The limestone was scoured flat and cracked by pressure. Over the last 12,000 years, acidic rainwater has deepened these cracks, creating the 'grykes' between the upstanding blocks, or 'clints'.*

Open plateau: *Pen-y-ghent rises above Moughton Scar and Crummack Dale*

Keep right along a grassier path; then left alongside an old wall to reach the **Beggar's Stile**. From here, drop steeply to a path across the open pastureland. Occasional leaning guideposts mark the route towards the stand of trees at **Crummack Farm** which soon comes into view.

5. Here, head through the gateway ahead-right; then join the course of the farm access road which snakes across the foot of the hillside, presently joining with another track from the left.

Keep ahead; beyond the junction to **Sowerthwaite Farm** the lane becomes tarred. In another 200 metres use the fingerposted gate on the right, a path for Norber. Thread with the path across the hillside; beyond a fallen stone stile you'll reach a high step stile. Turn left off this to a nearby fingerpost and go right to visit the scattered **Norber Stones**.

Gigantic boulders balanced on delicate pedestals of limestone; the Norber Stones recall when the great ice-sheet retreated back across the limestone plateau. In its wake were left stranded huge blocks of stone, gouged by the advancing ice from higher up Crummack Dale to the

north. Acid rain and outwash lowered the surface of the plateau much more quickly than dissolving the harder greywacke rock, leaving these massive marbles as a conundrum, glacial erratics famed across the geological world.

6. Return to the fingerpost and turn right. Swing left beyond the next stile, heading for walled **Thwaite Lane**. Join this and turn right to walk back to **Clapham**, arriving via tunnels beneath the estate of **Ingleborough Hall**. ♦

Three Peaks Challenge

This area of the Dales is known as the Three Peaks. The summits of Ingleborough and Pen-y-ghent are shapely headcorns of hard, resistant gritstone; isolated flat-topped peaks which take the eye from miles around. Highest of the three, Whernside is a whaleback mountain beyond Ingleborough. Taking in all three summits in one day, the Three Peaks Challenge is a 40 kilometre circuit involving 1,600 metres of ascent.

Sunlight illuminates the wood panelled interior of the George & Dragon, in Dent

George & Dragon, Dent

Astonishing views to the Howgill Fells and a tranquil riverside return to Dent's quaint old village lanes

What to expect:
Good, maybe muddy paths and tracks. Steady climb to start

Distance/time: 8km/ 5 miles. Allow 2½ -3 hours

Start/finish: Car park (pay & display) in Dent village

Grid ref: SD 704 871

Ordnance Survey Map: Explorer OL2 Yorkshire Dales: *Southern & Western areas: Whernside, Ingleborough & Pen-y-ghent*

The Pub: The George & Dragon, Main Street, Dent, Sedbergh, Cumbria LA10 5QL | 015396 25256 | www.thegeorgeanddragondent.co.uk

Walk outline: A lane rising from Dent's memorable mix of cobbles, cottages and ginnels soon narrows to a steep, wooded track beside waterfalls before gaining an old moorland roadway curling across Towns Fell. Marvellous views across Dentdale reward before a bridlepath drops into Deepdale and a riverside return on the Dales Way to Dent.

The **George & Dragon** *commands a corner at the heart of the quaint village. This traditional pub, all panels and log fires, appeals to all-comers, from weary ramblers to sports fans and family groups, with a suite of rooms in which to quaff Dentdale-brewed real ales. The nearby Sun Inn is also a treat.*

Sun Inn sign

▶ The George & Dragon at a glance

Open: Daily, 10.30am-11pm; 12-10.30pm Sundays
Brewery/company: Dent Brewery
Real ales: Dent Brewery beers plus guests
Food: Daily 12-2.30pm and 6pm-9pm. A quality, wide-ranging menu; some dishes cooked in Dent beers
Rooms: Ten en-suite rooms
Outside: None
Children & dogs: Children and dogs welcome

The Walk

1. Choose the road opposite the car park entrance, which climbs past cottages to the village green. Keep ahead up the 'No Through Road'. Beyond a final cottage the lane deteriorates to a stony track, signed as a bridleway to '**Flintergill**', a terrific, steep wooded cleft.

On the left in just a few metres a side path drops to a slabby riverbed, known locally as **Dancing Flags**. *Local weavers used to spread out their cloth here and 'waulk' it — wash, de-grease and felt the material.*

Return to the track and wind through a gate.

Just a short distance further up the track is a tree with an undercut root system — the **Wishing Tree**. *Folklore has it that if you pass through the root-bole gap three times in a clockwise direction you'll be granted a wish; do it widdershins (anticlockwise) and you'll have bad luck!*

The track climbs consistently within the woodland fringe. Immediately before the gate take the chance to divert right to the stone barn.

This old building at **High Ground farmstead** *is packed with old agricultural machinery and implements plus a display of old photographs of Dentdale's farming community. Nearby is a restored limekiln. One of many dotted across the Dentdale hillsides, it produced lime from roasting*

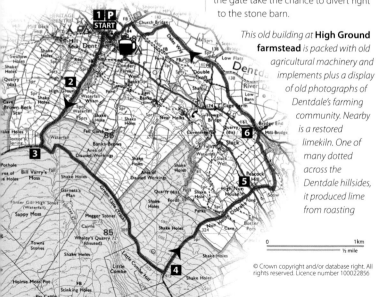

0   1km
½ mile

Sun, light and shadow: *Dent's quaint cobbled streets lead to the old Sun Inn*

limestone, put to many uses in industry, farming and household maintenance.

2. Continuing uphill, the woodland peels away at the next gate; divert right 50 metres to the little knoll to find a **toposcope** identifying the highlights of the extraordinary views from here. Return to the track and continue up to a T-junction.

3. Turn left on this old walled track, called **Occupation Road**.

The walls here are straight in comparison to the smaller, higgledy-piggledy ancient fields in the valley. This results from the Enclosure Acts of the 19th century, when the common land of the moors was 'taken in' from the wild by farmers intent on land improvement. This old droving road became important access for such farmers who 'occupied' these intakes of land.

The rutted track undulates across the fellside, with great views ahead of Whernside, one of the famous Three Peaks of the Yorkshire Dales, beloved of geography and geology teachers.

Secluded splendour: *The Howgills rise beyond verdant Dentdale*

Local geology was an interest of Adam Sedgwick, son of the Vicar of Dent. He became an academic at Cambridge, where his studies in stratigraphy revolutionised geology. One of his students was Charles Darwin.

4. At the next T-junction turn left, a rougher walled track signed for 'Nun House Outrake'.

Here's where the views across Dentdale come into their own. The northern slopes are dissected by short, wooded gills, each plugged by a stone or whitewashed farmhouse at its foot. To your left the shapely upwellings of the Howgill Fells are a study in landscape perfection, draping the horizon like a giant croissant.

Pass by the house at **Nun House**, dropping down the concreted driveway to reach a tarred lane.

5. Cross straight over and use three gates in-series through the farmyard area, continuing down the right edge of a pasture. Turn left through the handgate above the ruined **Scow farmhouse**; the waymarked path falls across the pasture to a handgate. Pass a limekiln and keep above the old wall-

line beyond this, looking for a higher handgate into a continuing pasture. Some 75 metres before a rebuilt cross-wall look right for a road bridge over **Deepdale Beck**; drop to this.

6. Don't cross the bridge; instead look left for the waymarked riverside footpath which now accompanies the beck, then the **River Dee** back to **Dent Bridge**. Turn left to the village. ◆

The 'Terrible knitters'

Dentdale was famed for its knitwear, popular with the military from Napoleonic times onwards. Such was the almost manic speed and skill of the craftspeople that they became known as the 'Terrible knitters' of Dent, a badge of honour worn with pride. The last such knitters both died in 2007, ending a venerable tradition.

FREE HOUSE

CRAVEN ARMS

THE
CRAVEN
CRUCK BAR

Golden days at the Craven Arms in Appletreewick

Craven Arms, Appletreewick

Along moorland tracks, beckside paths, Troller's Gill and the Dales Way beside the Wharfe, near Burnsall

What to expect:
One climb; good tracks and paths; rough going in Troller's Gill

Distance/time: 11km/ 7 miles. Allow 3½-4 hours

Start: Burnsall village green

Grid ref: SE 033 612

Ordnance Survey Map: Explorer OL2 Yorkshire Dales: *Southern & Western areas: Whernside, Ingleborough & Pen-y-ghent*

The Pub: The Craven Arms, Appletreewick, nr. Skipton BD23 6DA | 01756 720270 | www.craven-cruckbarn.co.uk

Walk outline: A gradual climb from the River Wharfe at Burnsall gains the moors and superlative views from Appletreewick Pasture. From here thread past mining remains and down stunning Troller's Gill gorge to peaceful Skyreholme and Appletreewick's rambler-friendly pubs. Return on the Dales Way beside the Wharfe to Burnsall.

Time-worn flagged floors, fire-bright blackened ranges, gas-lighting, wizened beams and a compact taproom featuring pub games such as table-skittles and ring-the-bull: The **Craven Arms** *enthrals at the fringe of the tiny village of Appletreewick, near the end of the walk.*

Way-side thirst quencher

▶ The Craven Arms at a glance

Open: Daily, 11.30am to 11pm. May vary, ring to confirm
Brewery/company: Free house
Real ales: Dark Horse, Moorhouses, Ilkley and other microbreweries. Also real ciders.
Food: Daily, 12-2.30pm and 6pm-9pm (all day from noon Fri-Sun)
Outside: Tables overlook the Wharfe Valley and Simon's Seat
Children & dogs: Very child and dog-friendly

The Walk

(**NB:** After prolonged heavy rain this walk may be flooded after Point 4. In this case return to the moorland track in Point 3 and turn down this, following it to rejoin the route below Troller's Gill at Point 5).

1. From Burnsall's **Red Lion Inn**, cross the bridge to find the waymarked **Dales Way** on your right. Cut half-left across the meadow, walking downstream beside the **River Wharfe**. The path shortly leaves the riverside to cross a narrow wooden footbridge; beyond this turn left up the farm road to reach a narrow lane.

2. Join the gated track opposite, soon accompanying a wall to your left. The track becomes enclosed before reaching wooden barns. Bear left after the gate,

remaining on the main stony track over junctions and across **Appletreewick Pasture**, an area of limestone moor pock-marked by conical sink-holes.

These mark where slightly acidic rainwater has pooled and eaten into the very porous, easily-dissolved limestone. Fissures become widened and unstable, leading to collapse of the land's surface into these definitive hollows in the landscape.

The track rises slightly; off to your right is the distinctive ridge of **Simon's Seat** whilst ahead is **Fancarl Crag** on Grimwith Fell. To your left lines of fells litter the horizon across the southern Dales. The old track eventually reaches a gate into a tarred lane across the moors.

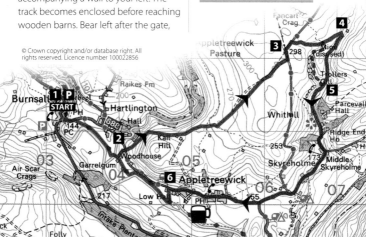

Dry stream bed: *Entering the spectacular narrow gorge of Troller's Gill*

At the fringes of the tarmac are sections of narrow-gauge railway and a grassy embankment stretching ahead.

The track originally served the nearby Gillhead mines, exploiting veins of lead at the head of Troller's Gill. A little steam engine hauled the calcite and fluorite ore to crushing and separating tanks on the moor. After closure around the Great War, the workings were reopened in the 1920s to provide fluorite to the steel industry, finally closing only in the 1980s.

3. Turn left on the lane. Beyond the bend take the stile, right, for 'Skyreholme'. A paved stretch gives way to a path across the tussocky moor, shortly reaching an area of old diggings. Keep left of these, a yellow-topped post confirming the way down to a wider moorland track. Go ahead, downhill to the sharp-right bend in 50 metres. The way is ahead off this bend on a grassy path rising past a marker post (staying on the wide track brings you to the old **Gillhead mine workings**; this is the flood route). Drift left above this post on a well-worn path across this low rise,

Bubbling beck: *A delightful path emerges from Troller's Gill*

dropping to a ladder stile and then a bridge over lively **Skyreholme Beck**.

4. Cross and turn right, presently entering the defile of **Troller's Gill**. Normally the waters sink underground at the entrance to this sheer-sided gorge, leaving an easy scramble down the ravine, which is popular with rock-climbers.

Troller's Gill is named after trolls which folklore says lived in the caves and hollows in the gorge. It's also haunted by the spectre of a huge, black hound with saucer-sized red eyes, the Barguest. If this ghostly beast is seen it foretells a death is imminent!

At the foot of the ravine keep ahead on the path.

5. The beck soon reappears from springs (the flood route also rejoins here) as you head down past the remains of a dam that once supplied water to nearby Skyreholme Mill, a cotton, then paper mill demolished in the 1970s. The path reaches a lane at the entrance to **Parcevall Hall.** Turn right; at the next junction turn right past the telephone

box and walk the very quiet lanes, as signposted, through to '**Appletreewick**' and the **Craven Arms** pub, 200 metres past the **New Inn**.

6. Some 400 metres past the pub turn left on the waymarked path before a caravan/camping site. Upon reaching the riverbank turn right and follow the **Dales Way** to **Burnsall** to complete the walk. ♦

Monks' rest?

Parcevall Hall stands secluded in beautifully landscaped grounds just a short way below the mouth of Troller's Gill. Originally a lodging house for peripatetic monks from Fountains Abbey inspecting their sheep farms hereabouts, the partly 16th-century building again became a religious retreat in 1963. Today, the 24 acres of gardens are open to the public between April and October.

The Falcon Inn, seen across the village green

The Falcon, Littondale

Two villages and two memorable pubs are linked on this easy stroll in tranquil Littondale

Distance/time: 7.5km/ 4¾ miles:. Allow 2½ hours

Start/finish: Arncliffe village green

Grid ref: SD 932 718

Ordnance Survey Map: Explorer OL30 Yorkshire Dales: *Northern & Central areas: Wensleydale & Swaledale*

The Pub: The Falcon Inn, Arncliffe, Skipton, North Yorkshire BD23 5QE | 01756 770205 | www.thefalconinn.com

Walk outline: From Arncliffe, a lane strings along beautiful, barely-known Littondale, above the River Skirfare in a vale dappled with haymeadows. Litton itself is squeezed into a narrow neck of the dale; the pretty cottages and home-brew inn here mark the return point for a secluded path slung between river, woods and limestone crags.

A delectable survival of a totally unaltered village parlour pub, **The Falcon** *has simply furnished, compact rooms and a tiny bar at which Yorkshire beer is served from a pot jug. Look for the fossils and minerals in the back room, off the taproom.*

Hand painted inn sign

▶ The Falcon at a glance

Open: Daily, 12-3pm, 7-11pm (10.30pm Sundays)
Brewery/company: Free house
Real ales: Timothy Taylor Bitter
Food: 12 noon-2.30pm, evenings by arrangement. Renowned pies, unfussy bar snacks and great sandwiches
Rooms: Five rooms, some en-suite
Outside: Benches overlook the green
Children & dogs: Children and dogs welcome

The Walk

1. Face the inn and turn left, weaving along the green past the old village water syphon.

Arncliffe became 'Beckindale' when the original version of the television 'soap' Emmerdale was first broadcast in 1972; rechristened 'The Woolpack', the Falcon was the centre of village life.

At the far end turn left on the road signed for 'Litton', passing **St Oswald's church** in its picturesque setting beside the **River Skirfare**.

2. Beyond the bridge, bend left with the road for Litton and follow it for the next two miles. Apart from high-summer weekends it's usually a very quiet lane. There's a great view left up the precipitous side dale of **Cowside Beck**; nearer to hand the tree-dressed limestone crags fringing **Old Cote Moor** loom. The compact village of **Litton** is strung below waterfalls issuing from the deep cleft of Potts Beck; beyond the village, Plover Hill, part of Pen-y-ghent, forms the distant horizon.

A joy of this walk is a second notable pub. **The Queens Arms** *recovered from the brink of closure in 2011; its homely rooms, exceptional food and beers from its microbrewery mark a great half-way stop.*

3. Continue through the village; just past the red telephone box fork left down the tarred bridleway past cottages. Slip beside the garden wall, cross the narrow **footbridge** and turn left, heading via handgates for the tall pine tree. Walk beside the side-stream then turn left on the track; in a few metres go right at the fingerpost 'Arncliffe 2¼m'. Go left

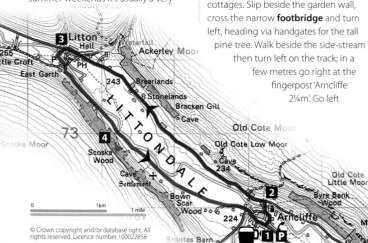

Country pub: *The unspoiled Queen's Arms at Litton is tucked into the dale*

through the next wall gap and follow the walked way, which soon becomes a rough path beside the Skirfare. The rocks and roots are awkward underfoot.

4. Pass the information board for **Scoska Wood.** Cross the waist of the meadow beyond, then a slim sleeper bridge over a beck well below a spectacular woodland-edge **waterchute.** A faint field track draws you ahead via handgates, heading for a large barn. Just before this, a gate leads into a rough track; this merges with a tarred lane. Continue ahead to **Arncliffe** to complete the walk. ♦

Water Babies

The Victorian author, the Reverend Charles Kingsley, regularly stayed in the village of Arncliffe. Local life seems to have inspired parts of his famous children's moral tale, The Water Babies, A Fairy Tale for a Land Baby, first published as a whole in 1863. It may well also have been the River Skirfare in Littondale into which Tom the chimney-sweep falls and drowns, before being transformed into a 'water baby'.

Fragrant wisteria decorates the front of The Bolton Arms, in Redmire

Bolton Arms, Redmire

An intricate walk linking Bolton Castle and the River Ure via pretty Redmire, deep in Wensleydale

What to expect:
Field paths, village lanes, farm tracks, short main road section

Distance/time: 7km/ 4½ miles. Allow 2½-3 hours

Start/finish: Castle Bolton, Bolton Castle (pay & display refundable by Castle visit)

Grid ref: SE 033 918

Ordnance Survey Map: Explorer OL30 Yorkshire Dales: *Northern & Central areas: Wensleydale & Swaledale*

The Pub: The Bolton Arms, Hargill Lane, Redmire, Leyburn, North Yorkshire DL8 4EA | 01969 624336 | www.boltonarmsredmire.co.uk

Walk outline: From the formidable medieval fortress of Bolton Castle, paths meander through Wensleydale haymeadows down to the charming village of Redmire, set around tranquil village greens. Lanes and tracks then fall to the river Ure and a riverside path to lively Redmire Force before climbing gently back to Redmire and the castle.

*At the edge of the pretty village of Redmire stands the creeper-clad old **Bolton Arms**, combining first-rate dining with a great welcome for ramblers in the beamed, match-boarded tap room, warmed by a woodburner, ideal for winter days. Beers from Yorkshire microbreweries often feature, whilst fresh Wensleydale produce is used in the kitchen.*

Woodburner warmth

▶ The Bolton Arms at a glance

Open: Daily, 11am-11pm
Brewery/company: Free house
Real ales: Black Sheep Bitter, John Smiths Bitter, guest beers
Food: 11.45am-2.15pm and 5.45pm-8.45pm, may vary; snacks all day
Rooms: Five en-suite rooms
Outside: Sheltered beer garden with great views over Wensleydale
Children & dogs: Children and dogs welcome

The Walk

1. Walk away from **Bolton Castle** along the long village green, lined with a veneer of old stone cottages.

Bear right before the green's end, past the village room and right at a fingerpost for 'Redmire'. Past the barn, skirt the field wall to a gap stile, left, for 'Redmire'. Aim to pass the tin barn in the next haymeadow. From the far bottom corner of the next pasture walk left beside the old railway embankment, reaching **Redmire Station** beyond a river footbridge. *Redmire Station hums with activity between Easter and October, when trains to and from Leeming Bar, 16 miles away, recall the heyday of the*

railway's peak between the wars. Redmire is the current western terminus of the heritage line; ambitious plans to relay the track to connect with the famous Settle & Carlisle line at Garsdale are in hand.

Turn downhill to **Redmire** and **The Bolton Arms**.

2. Walk to the village greens and **memorial cross**. Bear left up the road for Leyburn; within a few paces turning right on the signed public footpath beside **West Cottage**, through a handgate into meadow. Use a nearby handgate and head half-right, aiming for the distant church. Past a third handgate cut left across a small field, then ease right through more gates to a farm road. Turn right to quaint **St Mary's Church**.

3. Walk the tarred lane away from the church. In 150 metres use the gap-stile, left, and cross the pasture to **Well Lane**. Turn left on this and remain with it to its very end — don't be fooled by the 'false-end' gate, where the track continues left. Turn right, putting the **River Ure** on your left at the bank-foot, presently reaching the end of **Mill Lane**.

4. Keep ahead for the River Ure, walking upstream, then over an unusual footbridge to

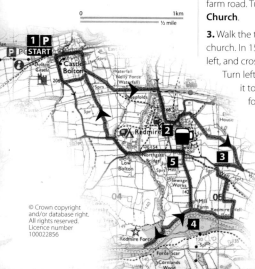

Summer river: *A gnarled ash tree frames the clear waters of the River Ure*

reach **Redmire Force**, a beautiful rake of falls. Return to Mill Lane and walk up to the village edge.

5. Go left on the main road, cross the bridge and bend right, then left. Take the second path on the right, for 'Castle Bolton'. Hug the wall to utilise three handgates; beyond the next gate above a small barn cut half-left to another gate, then right to cross the **old railway**. Rise ahead, then left to an offset corner and handgate. Keep uphill, looking for the gate beneath a tree, left, into a path through to a lane. Turn right to **Bolton Castle** to complete the walk. ♦

Bolton Castle

Bolton castle is an extraordinary fortress high above Wensleydale. It's the seat of Lord Bolton, a direct descendant of the original builder, Sir Richard le Scrope. Completed in 1399, the building reflects the transition between castle and residential manor, and was one of the earliest buildings in England to have chimneys. Mary Queen of Scots was imprisoned in exile here for six months in 1568, on the instructions of Elizabeth I.

Tall delphiniums edge the cobbled forecourt outside the Buck Inn

The Buck Inn, Malham

Tackle Malham's rivers and moor before reaching the spectacular twins of Gordale Scar and Malham Cove

What to expect:
Good paths and tracks, some boggy moorland, several short climbs

Distance/time: 10km/6¼ miles. Allow 3-4 hours

Start/finish: Malham village car park (pay & display)

Grid ref: SD 900 627

Ordnance Survey Map: Explorer OL2 Yorkshire Dales: *Southern & Western areas: Whernside, Ingleborough & Pen-y-ghent*

The Pub: The Buck Inn, Malham, near Skipton, North Yorkshire BD23 4DA | 01729 830317 | www.buckinnmalham.co.uk

Walk outline: The walk accompanies the lively headwaters of the River Aire south before rising on rough paths via Hanlith Moor to Weets Top and a panoramic view over North Yorkshire to distant Bowland and Pendle Hill. Wind then to the mouth of stunning Gordale Scar, before the awesome Malham Cove offers a memorable finale.

At the heart of the village, **The Buck Inn** *was rebuilt from a coaching inn in 1874 to serve Victorian visitors to the natural wonders of the area. Today's patrons are a mix of ramblers and cavers exchanging banter in the convivial Hikers Bar and families relaxing in the logfire-warmed, panelled lounge.*

Welcoming sign

▶ The Buck Inn at a glance

Open: Daily, 11am-11pm; 12noon-10.30pm Sunday
Brewery/company: Free house
Real ales: Beers from Wensleydale, Timothy Taylor and Theakston breweries
Food: Daily 12noon-3pm & 6pm-9pm; a strong menu of Dales-sourced ingredients — try the Malham & Masham Pie
Rooms: Twelve en-suite rooms
Outside: Patio; tables to front overlook the beck
Children & dogs: Children welcome, dogs allowed in Hikers Bar

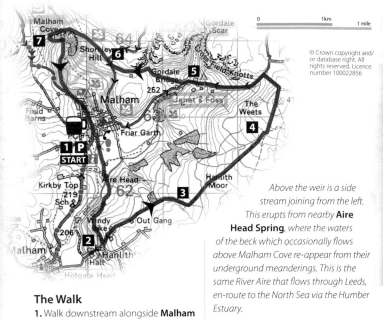

The Walk

1. Walk downstream alongside **Malham Beck**, water to your right. You're on the **Pennine Way**; the well-trodden path soon reaches a bend near a ruinous barn. Bear right off this bend on the path for 'Hanlith', still the Pennine Way. Possibly muddy pasture leads to **Black Hole Bridge** over **Gordale Beck**. Beyond here the path climbs easily uphill to the first of a number of gates to be used, one well-hidden beneath an ash tree at a wall-end. Down to your right the beck is harvested by a **weir** to fill some trout ponds.

*Above the weir is a side stream joining from the left. This erupts from nearby **Aire Head Spring**, where the waters of the beck which occasionally flows above Malham Cove re-appear from their underground meanderings. This is the same River Aire that flows through Leeds, en-route to the North Sea via the Humber Estuary.*

At a walled corner above a wooded bank and beyond a field gate the 'Pennine Way' is signed left. Follow this direction, gradually peeling away from the wall to use a gate above a converted barn. In a further 75 metres a handgate leads into a tarred lane at a sharp bend here at the top of **Hanlith**.

2. Turn uphill, swinging up this lane past the houses and barns at **Town Head**, immediately past which the route becomes a rough walled track

Wayside marker: *Three walkers inspect medieval Weets Cross*

called **Windy Pike Lane**. This undulates across the hillside, gaining height imperceptibly as ever-better views across the vale to the limestone hills, scars and cliffs above Malham offer a superb horizon.

3. Beyond a sharp-left bend the track reaches a gate into access land at the end of **Hanlith Moor**. For the first 200 metres the continuing track is obvious, but it soon peters out amidst the tussocky — and often boggy — moor.

Your target is the distinct low hilltop slightly-right, capped by a black-looking notch. Choose a way just right of this direction and you'll presently join a line of wall coming up from your right; continue to a gate at the walled corner.

These reedy moors are brimming with wildlife. In spring the marshy flushes are bursting with frog spawn. Look for the tumbling flight of lapwings, or 'peewits' and listen for the mournful cry of the curlew. If you're lucky you may also see a diminutive merlin hunting insects or spot a daylight-hunting short-eared owl.

On top of the world: *Walkers on the limestone pavement above Malham Cove*

4. Walk from the gate to the fingerpost 100 metres away; here turn left up the good track to a gateway near the 'trig' pillar at **Weets Top**. Commanding views all-round are the reward for this easy climb. The way down is along the gated, walled track beside the weather-worn **Weets Cross**.

The cross is a medieval monastic waymarker, guiding travellers on Fountains Abbey's vast sheep estate here. Only the base is original; the current cross shaft may have been moved from a nearby location.

The track drops to a tarred lane. Turn left and walk down to the sharp-left bend beyond **Gordale House Farm**. The well-made path into **Gordale Scar** is to the right here (extra one kilometre return).

5. The onward route is just round the corner and to the right over the old bridge, signed for 'Malham Cove'. The wallside path rises, offering great views into **Gordale Scar**. At one point a corner handgate puts the wall on your left, soon passing a stone barn. The path now curves right below wires to a lane.

6. Cross right to a ladder-stile and ahead on a stony track. In 300 metres drift left on a grassy track that heads for a distant

fingerpost beside a wall. Beyond here **Malham Cove** comes into view. The huge semicircle of cliff is topped by a serrated limestone pavement; beautiful, but difficult walking — and remember to keep well back from the edge.

7. At the far side locate the handgate and join the stepped path down into the valley. Follow the sandy path back to **Malham**, to complete the walk. ♦

Underground streams

Malham Cove's stunning curved cliff was created by a vast Niagara-like waterfall as glacial ice-sheets melted around 50-80,000 years ago. Strangely, the seasonal stream that flows well above the cove isn't the same one that appears from the base; the waters supplying this sink into the limestone moor about two kilometres northwest of the cove. Oddly, distant Aire Head Spring receives the waters from above the cove.

The Red Lion Inn, a memorable step back in time

Red Lion Inn, Langthwaite

An undulating walk in one of the most remote dales, with great views to savour and a superb riverside finalé

What to expect:
Lanes, tracks, moorland and riverside paths. Narrow stiles; very muddy after rain

Distance/time: 9km/ 5½ miles. Allow 3-3½ hours

Start/finish: Village car park, Langthwaite (pay & display)

Grid ref: NZ 005 025

Ordnance Survey Map: Explorer OL30 Yorkshire Dales: *Northern & Central areas: Wensleydale & Swaledale*

The Pub: The Red Lion, Langthwaite, Arkengarthdale, Richmond, North Yorkshire DL11 6RE | 01748 884218 | www.redlionlangthwaite.co.uk

Walk outline: A narrow lane threads to the hamlet of Booze, shortly followed by a steady climb up the flank of Fremington Edge. Grassy paths gain the ridgetop, from where exceptional views span the vast, dissected moorlands of the northern Dales. A steep zigzag descent leads to a peaceful path beside Arkle Beck, returning to Langthwaite through a mysterious short tunnel.

The **Red Lion Inn** *is a pint-sized period piece tucked away in tranquil Arkengarthdale. In the same hands for 50 years, the bar and snug are timeless treats, dotted with snaps recalling that favourite old TV series: 'All Creatures Great and Small'.*

Homely bar

▶ Red Lion Inn at a glance

Open: Daily, 11am-3pm and 7pm-11pm
Brewery/company: Free house
Real ales: Black Sheep Bitter plus other Black Sheep beers
Food: Snacks and crisps
Outside: Tables on a small paved patio beside the village 'square'
Children & dogs: Children welcome in family room; dogs not allowed

The Walk

1. Turn right from the car park; then right again at the turn for the village centre — there's a sign for the **Red Lion** high on a wall. The inn itself is just across the old bridge, a structure featured in 'A Woman of Substance' and other period drama productions. Follow the lane across the little square and wind uphill with it, a steep climb, initially through ashwoods, to the shoulder of land high above **Arkle Beck** where stands the secluded hamlet of **Booze**.

Booze is derived from an Old Norse word meaning 'house on a curved hillside'. The few farms and cottages here today at the end of the rough lane are a shadow of the 40 or so miners' houses which existed 150 years ago at the height of the lead mining industry here, when the sides of Slei Gill were riven by workings.

2. Locate **Town Farm** at the heart of the hamlet and turn right, through the two close-spaced gates beside the barn then keep ahead down the pasture. Beyond another gate drop to a waymarked path junction; turn right, then go left for 'Fremington', down the concrete access track and across a footbridge to reach **Storthwaite Hall Farm**.

3. Turn left immediately past the house up a walled bridleway for 'Hurst'. The walls peel back; trace the left-wall up to a gate through the cross-wall, use this

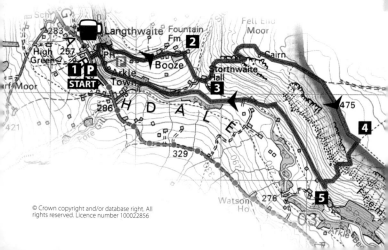

Verdant vale: *Arkengarthdale cleaves the backbone of England*

and turn right. The well-formed track is waymarked by yellow rectangles; it reaches a mined area (**Fell End lead mine**), at which point bend sharp-left to continue the climb. The slope eases as the track curves right, becoming a grassy trod marked by frequent cairns and riddled by rabbit burrows. *In early summer the tiny, delicate yellow blooms of mountain pansy glow in miniature drifts hereabouts.* Make your way to the tall cone-shaped cairn on the nearby hilltop.

From here a marvellous view across the deep gulch of Arkengarthdale is backed by the heights of Reeth Low Moor. Reeth is the village down to the left, with Swaledale beyond, whilst Arkengarthdale slides up towards the distant shadowy horizon of the highest fells of the North Pennines.

Return to the cairn-marked track and continue uphill to reach a gate at a walled corner beyond a marshy area. Pass through this and go ahead with the wall-side path which runs a good way away from the cliffs of **Fremington Edge**.

Upland architecture: *Traditional stone farmhouses and barns in Arkengarthdale*

Grouse moors stretch to your left; besides these game-birds you may well see curlew and meadow pipits and hear the supreme springtime song of skylarks. The immense view stretches to the distant North Yorkshire Moors.

In around 1 kilometre, the wall kinks distinctly left; be alert here for the small handgate through the fence-topped wall another 150 metres further along.

4. Use this gate and walk ahead across the reedy pasture, shortly reaching a cairn at the lip of plunging **Fremington Edge**. Your target is the walled track leading towards the farmhouse at the slope-foot directly below you. There is an old zigzag path down the scarp face; this passes through screes and boulderfields, a knee-jarring descent to reach the slope-foot wall at a gate and ladder-stile into the track.

5. Use neither; instead turn right alongside the wall, passing behind the nearer farmhouse at **Castle Farm**. Remain with this undulating path, presently beside a fence, for over 1 kilometre to the abandoned **Heggs House Farm**. Pass through the yard behind this, joining the grassy track

down to the bank of the **Arkle Beck**. Turn upstream, go through the nearby field gate (don't cross the bridge) and simply remain on the riverside path skirting haymeadows. Along the way is **Booze Wood tunnel**, after which the way becomes a firm track through sublime beech and Scots Pine woods before eventually emerging into **Langthwaite** square, to complete the walk. ♦

Mine tunnels

Booze Wood mine was the lowest of the string of workings based on Slei Gill; the tunnel here is probably a relic of the mine tramroad system connecting to crushing mills beside Slei Gill Beck. The mine opened in the 1870s but was never very profitable. It started as a a lead mine and later produced roofing flags, or stone tiles. A gushing sough, or mine drain, and fallen buildings remain hidden in the woods.

Useful Information

'Welcome to Yorkshire'
This comprehensive website draws together a wealth of information about visiting Yorkshire. **www.yorkshire.com**

Yorkshire Dales National Park
For in-depth information about the National Park, including 'What's on' listings of local events and tourist information. **www.yorkshiredales.org.uk**

Visitor Centres
Many towns in the area have Tourist Information Centres where staff will help with accommodation, heritage and outdoor activities. The main ones are listed here; there are also National Park Centres in some key locations.

Tourist Information Centres

Horton-in-Ribblesdale	01729 860333	horton@ytbtic.co.uk
Ingleton	01524 241049	ingleton@ytbtic.co.uk
Leyburn	01748 828747	ticleyburn@richmondshire.co.uk
Sedbergh	01539 620125	tic@sedbergh.org.uk
Settle	01729 825192	settle@ytbtic.co.uk
Skipton	01756 792809	skipton@ytbtic.co.uk

National Park Centres
Open daily April-October; limited in winter; closed in January

Aysgarth Falls	01969 662910	aysgarth@yorkshiredales.org.uk
Grassington	01756 751690	grassington@yorkshiredales.org.uk
Hawes	01969 666210	hawes@yorkshiredales.org.uk
Malham	01969 652380	malham@yorkshiredales.org.uk
Reeth	01748 884059	reeth@yorkshiredales.org.uk

Yorkshire Dales breweries and pubs
With around six microbreweries in the National Park and dozens more lapping the fringes, a torrent of excellent local beers flows from the handpulls of The Dales' pubs and inns. From Masham's ubiquitous *Black Sheep* to Settle's Lilliputian-sized *Three Peaks* brewhouse, there's a beer to satisfy every taste.

www.nwyorkscamra.co.uk and **www.keighleyandcravencamra.org.uk**

Weather
For the latest report for the Yorkshire Dales follow the link on the National Park website (see above) for 'Weather'. For details of local weather, go to **www.mylocalweather.org.uk** and click on the area you're interested in.